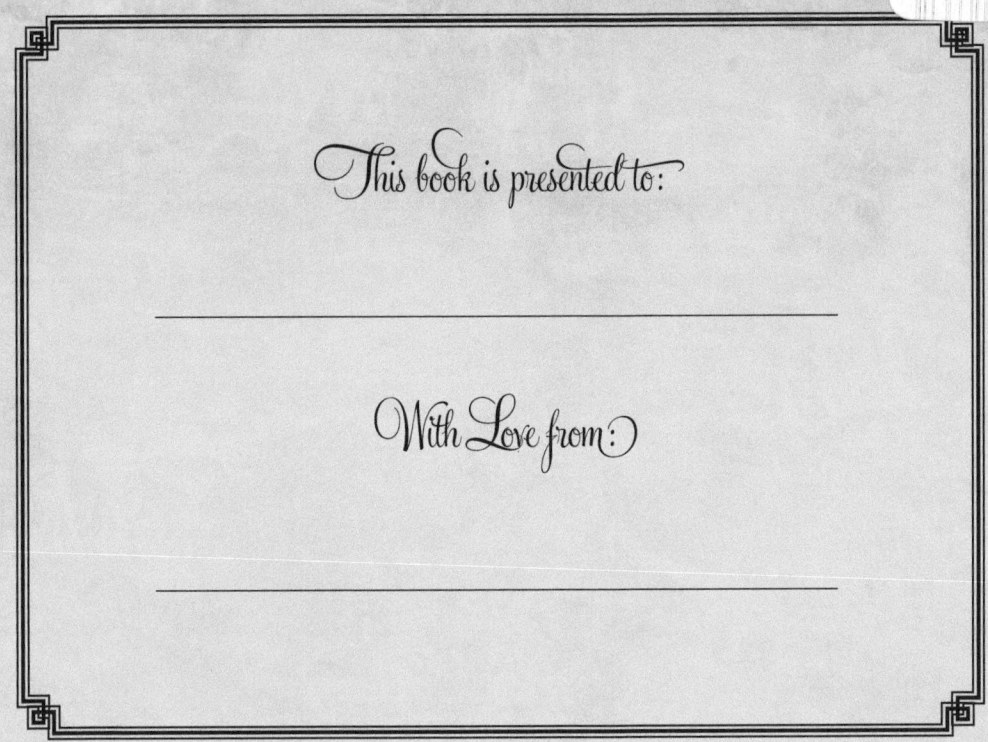

This book is presented to:

_____

With Love from:

_____

Introduction

The poems in this compilation are excerpts from *God's Grace: Psalms of Love, Laughter, Tears and Praise from Mother to Daughter*. This beautiful book was developed to give caregivers a means of expressing adoration for their chilldren and to remind "grown-up girls" that they are their Heavenly Daddy's Princesses. We are loved beyond measure!

There are so many negative influences that can degrade one's self esteem. Consider *God's Grace II* as a countermeasure filled with faith and favor, comfort and confidence. It is my prayer that this book will captivate the interest and imagination of the reader, reminding "Princesses" of all ages of their special gifts, particularly the gift of God's love and the love of those around them! We are blessed beyond measure!

Read these poems often and hide them in your child's heart. Please share your "God's Grace" experiences and feedback with us at christiangracepublishing@yahoo.com. Enjoy and continued blessings!

God's Grace II: Pearls of Love and Encouragement for Princesses of All Ages
Copyright © 2009 by Eurydice S. Stanley
Illustrations and graphics property of Christian Grace Publishing

Reprinted from *God's Grace: Psalms of Love, Laughter, Tears and Praise from Mother to Daughter*
TM & © Copyright 2006, Christian Grace Publishing

All rights reserved.

No part of this book may be reproduced, or transmitted in any form or by any means, electronic or mechanical, including photocopying, recording, or by any information storage and retrieval system, without written permission from the publisher.

For information, contact Christian Grace Publishing at ChristianGracePublishing@yahoo.com

God's Grace II: Pearls of Love and Encouragement for Princesses of All Ages First Edition published 2009

Library of Congress Cataloging-in-Publication Data
Stanley, Eurydice
God's Grace II: Pearls of Love and Encouragement for Princesses of All Ages
1. Children 2. Poetry 3. Parenting - Religious aspects - Christianity 4. Family & relationships - Parenting
5. Family and Relationships - General 6. Motherhood 7. Religion - Spirituality

ISBN - 0-9774468-3-2
13 Digit ISBN - 978-0-9774468-3-4

Library of Congress Control Number:2007905765

Printed in the United States of America

God's Grace II:
Pearls of Love and Encouragement for Princesses of All Ages

To all the World's Princesses,
especially Grace —
"God's Unmerited Favor"

Happy Birthday Angel!

Never Forget Mommy Loves You Very Much…

Always and All Ways!

This book is dedicated to Great-Grandma Bernice Rozell,
"Empress" of our royal family.

A portion of the proceeds from this book will support the **Emmarhaye P. Mitchell** Florida A&M University Army ROTC Cadet Scholarship Fund. We miss you Great-Grandma!

My Precious Jewel

Onyx eyes,
Ruby red lips,
Topaz skin,
Nails with opal tips…

You're a precious jewel…your treasures are yet to be discovered!

A champagne diamond unmasked,
Surviving nine months of pressure and darkness
You came out to the light shining,
Sparkling,
Incredibly captivating —
Every single facet of you.

Your Daddy and I watch in wonder,
Cherishing each brilliant sparkle
As we lovingly lift you on a pedestal of pride for display to the world…
A pedestal from which you will never come down, Sweet Princess.

Shine on,
Priceless, precious jewel —

Dazzle the world!

© Eurydice Stanley

Where Are You Going Busy Bee?

Where Are You Going Busy Bee?

Why won't you come and sit with me?

Life will soon fill your days with unimportant chores,

And people will try to convince you their job is yours!

Don't be fooled, my Darling —

Remember to stop and smell the roses…

Breathe deeply, my Sweet,

Know that <u>Living</u>, not *Doing* makes life complete!

© Eurydice Stanley

I Promise

I promise…

I will love you forever,

I will speak life into you,

I will treat you with respect,

I will support you,

I will be silly with you,

I will cry with you,

I would die for you,

I promise —

Always.

© Eurydice Stanley

Brown Sugar

"Brown Sugar Baby,"

    Your kisses taste so good,

        and you're so good to me!

Natural,

    Sweet,

        Granulated or hand-packed,

            You melt in extreme heat, so I must handle with care…

You dissolve within your surroundings,

    Making them better,

        More flavorful,

            And much more satisfying!

Brown Sugar, you're a natural complement to anything you touch

    Making it complete,

        Tasty,

           Tantalizing,

                And desired very much!

Sweet Brown Sugar Baby, you're so good!

© Eurydice Stanley

Heritage of Love
(For Grandma (Priscilla), Great-Grandma Mitchell and Great-Grandma Rozell)

People ask, "How is it that you speak of your baby with such love and esteem?"

Mommy always wonders, "What do you mean?"

You see —

Mommy heard these words from her Mommy and Grandmas as a little girl,
    She was often told she was the best in the whole world!

So it is quite natural (and true) for Mommy to say
    Words of love and encouragement to you each day.

Mommy knows you're brilliant, bold, without boundary and beautiful, it's true…
    Succeed or fail, Princess, your family will always love you!

There is nothing you can't do,
    And nothing from which you'd be discouraged (unless it was harmful for you).

"Go get 'em Tiger,"
    You'll go far —
        Your family is completely behind you, Honey,
            Go out and be the winner that you are!

© Eurydice Stanley

Sweet Butterfly Kisses

Your long curved eyelashes reach the sky,

Perfect for butterfly kisses from your eye!

But since you're still young,

Mommy will ensure

That your sweet Butterfly Kisses come from her!

I say "Butterfly Kisses" and you giggle with glee,

Because you know you'll soon be tickled by Mommy!

I pull you close and whisper in your ear

"Butterfly Kisses are here!"

Flit, Flutter, Flutter —

A delightful squeal — another kiss landed!

Yet another successful attack by Mommy,

"The Butterfly Kiss Bandit!"

© Eurydice Stanley

Daddy's Girl, Mommy's Baby

Daddy lets you have your way,

He's your personal jungle-gym for play.

You squeal with joy should he come near, but if you shed a tear…

    It's Mommy you want,

        Mommy you call,

            Mommy you reach for,

                Especially should you fall.

Yes, you're God's child —

    Daddy's girl,

        And Mommy's baby,

            The best of all possible worlds,

                For one special little lady!

© Eurydice Stanley

You Are Perfect for Nibbling!

Oh how big, sweet and juicy you are!

Dimpled elbows,
Dimpled knees,
Big round tummy —
Chubby cheeks!

Toes made for chewing,
Thunder thighs,
I know a neck is in there somewhere —
Between your shoulders and your eyes!

Mommy's big baby —
Tall, stocky and strong…
Mommy could nibble and kiss on you all day long!

© Eurydice Stanley

Yes, I'm a Princess!

Yes, I'm a Princess —
    Both my Daddy's are Kings,
        And I enjoy the favor their special status brings.
As a child of the Heavenly King
    I am heir,
        To treasures beyond imagination,
            And intrinsic riches beyond compare!
My Heavenly Father created all,
    And said I am His seed —
My earthly Daddy provides guidance and monitors my every step,
    He provides two strong arms to hold on to during my time of need.
My Mommy is a Queen —
    And prepares me to take my rightful place on the throne —
My riches are not measured by wealth,
    But by love and happiness alone!
I'm a royal heir —
    My parents come from a royal, heavenly line,
        Ensuring I'll have thousands of blessings from now until the end of time!
Hope this clarifies my lineage —
    And explains why I seem,
        Happy all the time,
            and filled with joy and glee!
Yes, I'm blessed by birthright and faith —
    But my blessings can be yours too!
        Confess faith in God — give Him your life —
            And you'll be royalty too!

© Eurydice Stanley

About The Artists

Author, Eurydice S. Stanley thanks God daily for His love, Grace, mercy and the gift of motherhood. She is the proud Mommy of two of God's greatest promises given during times of crisis - Grace, age 7, a post 9/11 baby and Christian, a "hurricane souvenier" from the 2004 Florida hurricane season. She has served for more than 16 years in the military and is currently an active duty Army National Guard Officer. "Dr. Eurydice" is a Christian Counselor, Psychologist and Temperament Therapist. She travels across the country as a motivational speaker and is the founder of B.E.S.T. 2 Reign, an organization dedicated to promoting confidence and tenacity despite life's challenges. She and her children encourage participants to achieve their greatest potential and identify their purpose in life. Eurydice is a member of numerous organizations to include Alpha Kappa Alpha Sorority, Inc, the Association of the United States Army and is a lifetime member of the NAACP and Florida A & M University Association, her beloved alma mater. Eurydice has been nationally recognized for excellence in poetry. The Stanley family resides wherever the Army sends them, currently in Washington D.C.

Artist, Samantha Christian — Samantha Marie Christian, also known as "SCitz," is the only beloved daughter of Eugene and Claudette Christian of Homestead, Florida. A graduate of North Miami Senior High (2002), Samantha continued her education at Florida A&M University where she obtained a Bachelor's Degree in Fine Art (Drawing/Painting), Class of 2006. A talented musician and former Clarinet Section performer in the world renowned "FAMU Marching 100," Samantha is currently honing in on her dual talents, using art to capture what music cannot. "SCitz" won the prestigious Nationally Historically Black Colleges and Universities (HBCU) Art Competition sponsored by Verizon. She was selected as one of the talented artists to bring *God's Grace: Psalms of Love, Laughter, Tears and Praise from Mother to Daughter* to life in 2006.

Layout — Steve Parrish, EssP design — Steve is a graphic designer living in Northern Virginia with his wife and two wonderful daughters.

Graphic Illustration — Peter Hemmer — Peter is a graphic designer living in Melbourne, Florida with his wife and their triplets.

A Special Invitation

"For God so loved the world, that He gave His only begotten Son, that whosoever believeth in him should not perish, but have everlasting life."
John 3:16

Parenting is a blessing but it definitely has its challenges — I could not imagine trying to do this without God! If you have not sought the Father's Hand and Face, consider the life of both you and your child…God does not promise us anything except for peace and life everlasting, coupled with rest and safe haven in His loving arms.

If you're ready to give your life to Christ, simply pray this prayer:

"Father, I repent of my sins. Please forgive me and lead my life. I ask you into my heart, my life and my world. I know that you are my Lord and Savior, and I thank you for your sacrifices for me. I ask you to guide me and my family, and let us reflect your love here on earth. I thank you and I praise you for your grace and mercy!"

Welcome, friend to the body of Christ! Find a good church to facilitate your growth and guide you on your fantastic journey! I pray your continued strength and blessings! If you gave your life to Christ or have anything that you'd like to share after reading "God's Grace II," send comments to christiangracepublishing@yahoo.com or visit our website at www.dreurydice.com.

May the Lord continue to hold you in His arms!

Continued Blessings!

Ordering Information

For additional copies of "*God's Grace II: Pearls of Love and Encouragement for Princesses of All Ages*" or to obtain a copy of "*God's Grace: Psalms of Love, Laughter, Tears and Praise from Mother to Daughter,*" visit **www.dreurydice.com**.

To schedule Dr. Stanley, Grace and Christian for speaking engagements, please visit **www.dreurydice.com**.

Corporations and interested parties are encouraged to contact Christian Grace Publishing regarding the purchase and donation of copies of God's Grace II or other Christian Grace Publications at reduced rates to schools, shelters and non-profit organizations.

Thank you for sharing the gift of Grace, Hope and God's love with others.

www.ingramcontent.com/pod-product-compliance
Lightning Source LLC
LaVergne TN
LVHW071031070426
835507LV00002B/120

9 780977 446834